TABLE OF CONTENTS

Novel-Ties® are printed on recycled paper.

For the Teacher

This reproducible study guide to use in conjunction with *The Hobbit* consists of lessons for guided reading. Written in chapter-by-chapter format, the guide contains a synopsis, pre-reading activities, vocabulary and comprehension exercises, as well as extension activities to be used as follow-up to the novel.

In a homogeneous classroom, whole class instruction with one title is appropriate. In a heterogeneous classroom, reading groups should be formed: each group works on a different novel at its reading level. Depending upon the length of time devoted to reading in the classroom, each novel, with its guide and accompanying lessons, may be completed in three to six weeks.

Begin using NOVEL-TIES for reading development by distributing the novel and a folder to each child. Distribute duplicated pages of the study guide for students to place in their folders. After examining the cover and glancing through the book, students can participate in several pre-reading activities. Vocabulary questions should be considered prior to reading a chapter; all other work should be done after the chapter has been read. Comprehension questions can be answered orally or in writing. The classroom teacher should determine the amount of work to be assigned, always keeping in mind that readers must be nurtured and that the ultimate goal is encouraging students' love of reading.

The benefits of using NOVEL-TIES are numerous. Students read goo literature in the original, rather than in abridged or edited form. The good reading habits, formed by practice in focusing on interpretive comprehension and literary techniques, will be transferred to the books students read independently. Passive readers become active, avid readers.

SYNOPSIS

Bilbo Baggins, a comfort-loving conventional hobbit is the unlikely hero of this mythic tale of high adventure. In a powerful struggle between good and evil, Bilbo, the wizard Gandalf, and thirteen dwarves fight to reclaim the lost treasures and kingdom of the dwarf Thorin. Through his luck and a variety of experiences, Bilbo learns to deal with increasingly difficult moral challenges.

Although he would have been content to spend his days in his comfortable burrow, Bilbo is persuaded by Gandalf to join his plot to rescue the dwarf treasure from the evil dragon, Smaug. The dwarves, after frolicking in Bilbo's home, eating all his food, and laughing at his expense, reluctantly accept him into their band.

Danger and adventures beset the group. Trolls capture Bilbo and the dwarves and they are saved only by Gandalf's wizardry. At Rivendell, the elf Elrond provides them with a map to find the Lonely Mountain. They are captured by goblins. Bilbo escapes only to find himself playing a game of riddles with the loathsome Gollum. But he discovers the ring which allows him to become invisible.

The dwarves are rescued from the goblins and Wargs by the Eagles of the Misty Mountains and taken with Bilbo to the home of Beorn, a skin changer. After resting and receiving good advice, the dwarves and Bilbo resume their quest: this time they go without Gandalf. They leave the path in Mirkwood, despite Beorn's warning, and are captured by giant spiders and then by wood-elves. Bilbo rescues the dwarves and hides them in barrels which are destined for Lake-town.

The Master of Lake-town and the men who live there provide safety and tell Bilbo and the dwarves that the downfall of Smaug has been prophesied. They leave for the Lonely Mountain where they find the Side-door and a thrush who helps them open it.

Bilbo, fearful, but with increasing courage, goes alone into Smaug's lair. Smaug, in an effort to destroy Lake-town, is himself destroyed. The men of Lake-town and the elves march on Lonely Mountain to share in the treasure which the dwarves believe belongs to them. Thorin sends for additional dwarves to help prepare for battle and denies the men of Lake-town any treasure.

Suddenly the men, elves, and dwarves are attacked by a vast army of goblins and Wargs. The gory Battle of Five Armies begins. Good defeats evil. Amends are made between the elves and dwarves, but Thorin has been killed. Bilbo Baggins returns home having refused most of his share of the spoils, but far richer in character and experience.

PRE-READING ACTIVITIES

1. Preview the book by reading the title and the author's name and by looking at the illustration on the cover. What do you already know about this book? Do you think it is a book of realistic fiction or fantasy? Do you expect the book to be amusing or serious?

2. The world of *The Hobbit* is inhabited by dwarves, trolls, elves, goblins, dragons, giants, wargs (wolves), and hobbits. These fantastic creatures are given human characteristics: they can sing, laugh, tell stories, eat, and drink. They are friendly, impetuous, and adventurous. Do you know of any people in real life or characters in fiction who share many of these characteristics?

3. Norse and Old English mythology are the major sources of Tolkien's inspiration for *The Hobbit*. The names of the dwarves in the story come from Norse mythology. The adventures of the Hobbit parallel those of Beowulf. The young Scandinavian warrior Beowulf delivers Hrothgar the Dane and his people from the menace of the monster Grendel; in his old age he fights a victorious but fatal battle against a terrible dragon to save his people. What other myths or legends do you know where the forces of good overcome the forces of evil?

4. A quest in a medieval romance is the recounting of an adventurous expedition undertaken by a knight to gain an object or achieve a goal (e.g., the quest for the holy grail). As you read *The Hobbit*, determine how close it comes to its medieval predecessor.

5. Do some research to learn about the history of runes. The classical definition of a rune is "a secret." Certain runes represented the names of gods and were used to appeal to them. As you read *The Hobbit*, notice how Old English runes are used to evoke an atmosphere of magic, mystery, and antiquity.

6. **Social Studies Connection:** Look carefully at the map of Wilderland at the beginning of the book. Trace the path of the expedition as you read the book.

7. Family ancestry plays an important part in the action of this story. Draw a family tree and record the lineage in *The Hobbit* as you read the story. This will help you understand complicated relationships among characters.

8. **Cooperative Learning Activity:** Work with a small group of classmates to brainstorm and create a word web showing word associations for "hobbit" and words that sound like "hobbit." You may be interested to learn that one definition for the word "hob" is hobgoblin or elf. As you read the book decide whether your word associations are consistent with the hobbits in the story.

9. Since *The Hobbit* is not set in a specific historical period or geographical location, the place and time are left to your own imagination. The settings are forests, rivers, plains, and mountains which are richly described. Tolkien tells of the shrubs, trees, and flowers growing in each area. As you read, record changes in flora and fauna and prepare collages or drawings depicting settings and inhabitants you meet in the story.

CHAPTER I

Vocabulary: Draw a line from each word on the left to its meaning on the right. Then use the numbered words to fill in the blanks in the sentences below.

1. prudent
2. blunder
3. legendary
4. haughty
5. audacious
6. fragments
7. obstinately
8. remuneration

a. payment
b. mythical
c. stubbornly
d. parts broken off; small pieces
e. wise
f. showing great pride in oneself and disdain for others
g. daring
h. careless or stupid mistake

. . . .

1. I was accused of being _____ when I suggested we go skydiving on my birthday.

2. It is _____ to save part of your allowance each week.

3. Their enemy's strength was _____, causing the smaller army to flee in retreat.

4. After working overtime every night this week, I expected extra _____.

5. No matter how much we coaxed him, my little brother _____ refused to go to bed.

6. The servers at the new restaurant were so _____ that no one wanted to return for another meal.

7. I knew it was a(n) _____ to ask my aunt her age when I saw her blush and hesitate to answer.

8. The scientists could reconstruct an entire dinosaur just by finding _____ of its skeleton.

> Read to find out if Bilbo Baggins joins the elves.

Questions:

1. Why did Gandalf come to the home of Bilbo Baggins?

2. How did the dwarves lose their treasure?

3. What did you learn about Bilbo Baggins' character when the dwarves entered his home?

4. What awakened "Tookish" feelings inside Bilbo Baggins? What were some of the Tookish and some of the Baggin elements in Bilbo?

Chapter I (cont.)

5. What happened when Mr. Baggins turned the handle and went in?

6. How did Gandalf get Bilbo to agree to join the dwarves?

Questions for Discussion:

1. Would you like to meet a hobbit? Do you think a hobbit would be happy to meet you?

2. Is your own character more like that of the Baggins or the Tooks? Which kind of character do you seek as a friend?

3. Do you think Bilbo will be able to rise to the challenge presented to him?

Literary Devices:

I. *Point of View*—Point of view in literature refers to the voice telling the story. It could be one of the characters or the author as narrator. What is the point of view in this story?

_____

Why do you think the author chose this point of view?

_____

_____

_____

I. *SimIle*—A simile is a figure of speech in which a comparison between two unlike objects is stated directly, using the words "like" or "as." For example:

> The poor little hobbit could be seen kneeling on the hearth-rug,
> shaking like a jelly that was melting.

What is being compared?

_____

Why is this better than just saying, "the little hobbit was so nervous, he was trembling"?

_____

_____

Chapter I (cont.)

Literary Element: Reality *vs.* Fantasy

Use the chart below to show what seems real and what seems like fantasy in the world of hobbits. Why do you think there are some aspects of reality in the lives of the hobbits? Continue to add to this chart as you continue to read the book.

Reality	Fantasy

Writing Activities:

1. Imagine you are Bilbo Baggins and write a journal entry expressing your conflicting emotions on the day that the dwarves arrived at your home.

2. Bilbo made several statements which he later regretted. Write about a time when you made a statement you later regretted.

CHAPTERS II – IV

Vocabulary: Draw a line from each word on the left to its meaning on the right. Then use the numbered words to fill in the blanks in the sentences below.

1.	palpitate	a.	rob goods by force, especially in times of war
2.	deception	b.	ritual repetitions of charms or spells
3.	shirk	c.	thought of with respect; prized
4.	esteemed	d.	personal belongings; gear
5.	plunder	e.	shake; quiver
6.	gnash	f.	concealment; distortion
7.	incantation	g.	put off; avoid
8.	paraphernalia	h.	grind; strike together

. . . .

1. Knowing I would never _____ the responsibility, my friend trusted me to walk her dog each day she was gone.

2. I felt my heart _____ when I realized I didn't know any of the answers on the quiz.

3. The clown barely squeezed into the car with all the _____ necessary for his act.

4. A master of _____, the magician made it seem as if his subject had been sawed in half.

5. First the fierce dog began to _____ his teeth together, then he attacked.

6. Cold, hungry, and without shelter, the victims looked at the results of the _____ of their town.

7. The generous and caring couple were _____ by all who knew them.

8. As she stirred her bubbling brew, the witch uttered _____ to cast a spell upon her enemies.

> Read to find out why Bilbo and his fellow travelers stayed at Elrond's home for two weeks.

Questions:

1. Why did Bilbo follow the dwarves' commands?

2. Why might a hobbit such as Bilbo make an excellent burglar?

3. Why were the captured dwarves in great danger from the trolls?

4. What caused the trolls' downfall?

Chapters II – IV (cont.)

5. Why was Bilbo disappointed that Gandalf would not let him visit with the elves?

6. Why did the expedition stay at Elrond's home for as long as fourteen days?

7. What important clue did Elrond find, and what particular knowledge did he use to find it?

8. Why did the expedition take shelter in the cave?

9. Why were the goblins furious when they saw the sword Thorin had worn?

Questions for Discussion:

1. Did you find the trolls to be a frightening threat, a humorous diversion, or both?

2. Do you think the dwarves and Bilbo will ever return to claim the treasure they plundered from the trolls?

3. What special qualities do you think Gandalf possessed which enabled him to rescue his friends?

Literary Devices:

I. *Personification*—Personification refers to a literary device in which the author endows inanimate objects with human qualities or actions. For example:

> Boulders, too, at times came galloping down the mountain-sides,
> let loose by midday sun upon the snow. . .

What is being personified?

_____

How does this help you visualize the scene?

_____

_____

Find another example of personification. Provide page number.

_____

_____

Chapters II – IV (cont.)

II. *Foreshadowing*—Foreshadowing refers to the clues an author provides to suggest what will happen later in the story. What did the following passage foreshadow?

> That, of course, is the dangerous part of caves: you don't know
> how far they go back, sometimes, or where a passage may lead
> to, or what is waiting for you inside.

_____

_____

Art Connection:

Tolkien never described the appearance of the goblins. Use your imagination to draw a goblin. Compare our imagined goblins with those of your classmates.

Writing Activity:

Use the device of personification to enhance a written description of a scene that is familiar to you.

Chapters II – IV (cont.)

Literary Element: Characterization

Use the diagram below to compare the characteristics of hobbits, dwarves, trolls, elves, and goblins. Record the characteristics they have in common in the center circle.

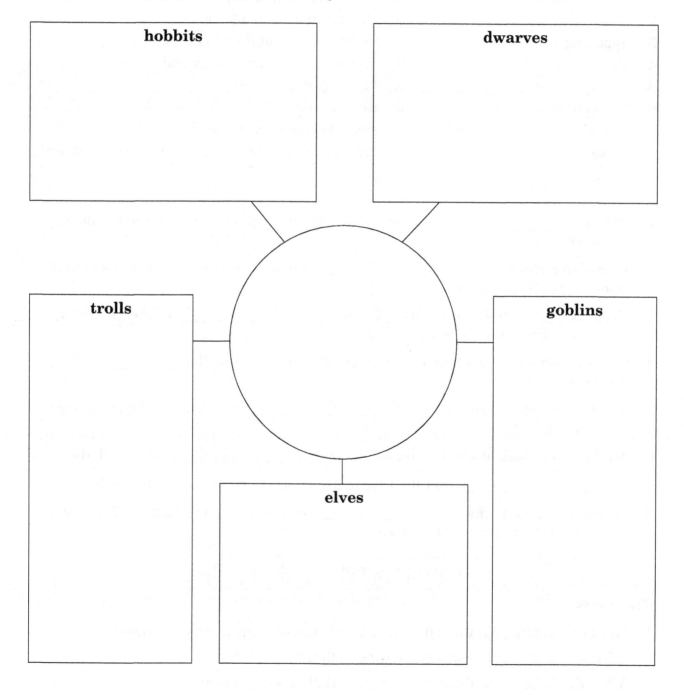

CHAPTERS V – VII

Vocabulary: Draw a line from each word on the left to its definition on the right. Then use the numbered words to fill in the blanks in the sentences below.

1.	subterranean	a.	belonging to the past; not modern
2.	antique	b.	causing dismay or horror
3.	appalling	c.	undergoing mental or emotional strain
4.	stark	d.	area overgrown with ferns and shrubs
5.	trestle	e.	harsh; grim; desolate
6.	bracken	f.	underground
7.	morsel	g.	small bite or portion, as of food
8.	tense	h.	bridge made of horizontal bars resting on A-frames

. . . .

1. We felt the _____ sway beneath our feet as we walked across during the storm.

2. Everyone huddled in the _____ tunnels, hoping to protect themselves from the approaching tornado.

3. Even though I was well prepared, I became _____ as the moment of the gymnastics competition drew near.

4. There wasn't a tree or a flower to brighten the appearance of the _____ landscape.

5. I prefer the charm and coziness of _____ furniture to the efficiency of new objects.

6. My dog is so small, it survives on only a(n) _____ of food each day.

7. The _____ hid the long-unused road to our cabin in the woods.

8. No one could forget the _____ scene of overturned cars and wounded passengers at the site of the accident.

> Read to find out how Bilbo benefits from the ring.

Questions:

1. In what condition did Bilbo find himself when he regained consciousness?
2. Why did Bilbo play a riddle game with Gollum?
3. What did Bilbo learn about the ring from Gollum's mutterings?
4. How did Bilbo escape from the dark place?
5. Why did Gandalf have a strong allegiance toward Bilbo?

Chapters V – VII (cont.)

6. Why didn't Bilbo tell the dwarves about the magic ring?

7. Why did the wolves flee from the area where the dwarves were hiding?

8. How did Bilbo and the dwarves escape the fire in the trees?

9. What caused Gandalf to decide that it was time to leave the quest?

10. Why was Beorn called a "skin changer"?

11. Why was Beorn willing to help Gandalf and the others?

Questions for Discussion:

1. Which magical creature that you have come upon in the story so far is the scariest? Which is the most likeable?

2. Why do you think the author found it necessary to have Gandalf leave the expedition?

3. What do you think Bilbo had achieved through his trait of cleverness?

4. Do you think that Bilbo and the dwarves will accomplish their goal without Gandalf to help?

Literary Element: Characterization

Use a chart, such as the one below, to provide examples of the growth in wisdom, courage, and initiative shown by the dwarves and by Bilbo.

	Dwarves	**Bilbo**
wisdom		
courage		
initiative		

Writing Activities:

1. Reread the first two pages of Chapter VII. Using this descriptive passage as a model, write your own descriptive passage in which you imagine you are flying over and landing in your neighborhood.

2. Write about a goal or a destination that you wish to reach. Enumerate the skills which would allow you to achieve this. Explain whether you think you can reach this goal and how its achievement might change your life.

CHAPTERS VIII – X

Vocabulary: Use the context to figure out the meaning of the underlined word in each of the following sentences. Compare your definitions with dictionary definitions.

- As Bilbo's sharp <u>inquisitive</u> eyes became used to the dark, he could see the dwarves hiding behind the trees.
- Bombur continued to sleep with a smile on his face, no longer caring for all the problems that <u>vexed</u> them.
- The <u>portcullis</u> was often open, allowing a lot of traffic to go in and out near the water-gate.
- The wine was so <u>potent</u> it made the wood-elf drowsy.
- An <u>ominous</u> nod in the direction of the mountain signaled to us that there was a dangerous dragon lurking there.
- The Master, looking forward to peace in the land, wished for no <u>enmity</u> between himself and the more powerful Elvenking.

Word	Your Definition	Dictionary Definition
1. inquisitive		
2. vexed		
3. portcullis		
4. potent		
5. ominous		
6. enmity		

> Read to find out how the elves are rescued.

Questions:

1. Why did the Hobbit and dwarves neglect to follow the advice given by Beorn and Gandalf?
2. What role did luck play in the rescue of the dwarves?
3. What experiences in the forest caused Bilbo to have an improved self-concept?
4. What misunderstanding caused the dwarves to be imprisoned?
5. Why didn't Thorin want the Elvenking to know about his quest?
6. What was Bilbo's first job a a burglar?
7. Describe Bilbo's plan for escape. When did luck help?

Chapters VIII – X (cont.)

8. What news did Gandalf receive that made him decide to rejoin Bilbo?

9. What were the attitudes of the inhabitants of Lake-town toward Thorin's mission? How did their attitudes compare with those of their Master and of the Elvenking?

10. Why did the Master help Thorin and his group? How did he help them?

Questions for Discussion:

1. What special qualities do you think Bilbo and Thorin possessed that caused them to emerge as leaders of the group?

2. In Chapter Eight, Tolkien wrote, ". . . if Bilbo had had the sense to see it. . ." What do you think Tolkien meant by this statement?

3. Who do you think had a more realistic attitude toward the mission—Bilbo or the dwarves?

Literary Element: Characterization

Bilbo had many skills which emerged during his experiences in the forest. Use the chart below to describe some of them and tell how they helped him.

Bilbo's Skill	How It Helped

Writing Activity:

Imagine you are Bilbo Baggins. Choose one of your adventures and write a journal entry describing your thoughts and feelings immediately after the adventure ended.

CHAPTERS XI – XIII

Vocabulary: Analogies are equations in which the first pair of words has the same relationship as the second pair of words. For example: COMEDY is to TRAGEDY as COMMENCE is to CONCLUDE. Both pairs of words are opposites. Choose the best word from the Word Box to complete each of the analogies below.

WORD BOX			
coward	lair	pallid	waning
crannies	marauding	perilous	

1. INCREASING is to DECREASING as WAXING is to _____.

2. BEAR is to DEN as COUGAR is to _____.

3. CAREFUL is to CAUTIOUS as DANGEROUS is to _____.

4. HEALING is to DOCTORS as _____ is to BANDITS.

5. FORESTS is to WOODS as _____ is to CREVICES.

6. VIBRANT is to _____ as BRAVE is to COWARDLY.

7. CRINGED is to _____ as NAPPED is to DOZED.

> Read to find out how Bilbo acquired the Arkenstone.

Questions:

1. What happened to permit Thorin to fit the key into the hole? What rune and moon letters letters prophesied this?

2. How did the dwarves let Bilbo down? How did Bilbo differ from the dwarves?

3. What was meant by "the desire of dwarves"?

4. What was the one useful thing that Bilbo learned as a result of his second encounter with the dragon?

5. Why did Bilbo take the Arkenstone? What were his feelings when he took it?

6. Why did the dwarves take so much treasure from the dragon's lair?

7. Why did the dwarves and Bilbo leave the palace? How did Balin and Thorin know how to escape?

Chapters XI – XIII (cont.)

Questions for Discussion:

1. What enabled Bilbo to become so brave?

2. What is true courage?

3. What was the real battle Bilbo fought in the tunnel?

Writing Activity:

Bilbo calls himself by many names. Use the chart below to describe the adventure that led to each name. The first one has been done for you.

Bilbo's Name	Adventure
Clue-finder	discovery of the knocking thrush at the tunnel-gate
Web-cutter	
Stinging fly	
Chosen for the lucky number	
Buries his friends alive	
No bag went over me	
Friend of bears	
Guest of eagles	
Ringwinner	
Barrel-rider	

Now write about an adventure you might have. Choose an appropriate name for yourself.

CHAPTERS XIV – XVI

Vocabulary: Use the words in the Word Box and the clues below to solve the crossword puzzle.

WORD BOX			
amends	coveted	eminent	laden
bade	decrepit	foiled	prophecies
benefactor	dreary	foreboding	

Across

2. one who gives financial or other aid

5. predictions; revelations

8. foretelling; giving warning

10. past tense of bid

11. reparations or payments made as satisfaction for insult or injury

Down

1. weakened by old age, illness or hard use

3. towering above others; outstanding

4. prevented from being successful

6. weighed down with a load

7. wished for excessively

9. gloomy

Chapters XIV – XVI (cont.)

> Read to find out if Bilbo wants to continue or end his quest.

Questions:

1. What did the burglar's title "Barrel-rider" indicate to Smaug?

2. Bard showed his skill and intelligence by instructing the villagers to cut the bridges and by slaying the dragon. What part did his lineage play in his success?

3. Why did the Master reveal that "I am the last man . . ." Of whom is he speaking? Why did he make this statement at this particular time?

4. What were the differences between the Master and Bard? What leadership qualities did each have? Who killed Smaug?

5. Why did the Elvenking decide to leave home and travel to Esgarath?

6. Why was Bilbo willing to end his quest with the killing of Smaug, while Thorin was not?

7. What did Bombur mean when he said that Thorin was a dwarf with a stiff neck?

Questions for Discussion:

1. What do you think of the advice given to Thorin by Roac, son of Carc? Would you have followed the advice? Reviewing all that has happened so far, evaluate Bard's position. Do you agree with his requests? How does his approach to Thorin compare with Thorin's responses? What qualities of leadership did both display?

2. In handing over the Arkenstone to Bard, Bilbo exhibited the most noble kind of heroism. Discuss Bilbo's character. What character traits permitted this act of nobility?

Writing Activity:

Think about some real people you know or have read about who are leaders. What qualities of leadership do they display? Choose one person and write a character sketch about that person in which you describe leadership qualities as well as other characteristics.

CHAPTERS XVII – XIX

Vocabulary: Choose the best word from the Word Box to complete each of the analogies below.

WORD BOX		
alter	content	ponder
casket	onslaught	wrath

1. BRAID is to PLAIT as CHANGE is to _____.

2. TRUMPET is to BRASS as _____ is to WOOD.

3. ANGER is to _____ as CONFUSION is to BEWILDERMENT.

4. DECEIT is to HONESTY as CONCLUDE is to _____.

5. SURRENDER is to _____ as GATHER is to DISPERSE.

6. _____ is to ECSTATIC as SAD is to DEPRESSED.

> Read to learn how the Battle of Five Armies turned out.

Questions:

1. What did Thorin promise Bard in exchange for the Arkenstone?

2. Why did Dain's army attack first?

3. Why did the Elvenking set aside his anger at Thorin and decide that he would not begin a war for gold?

4. Why did Dain agree to join with Bard and the Elvenking when Gandalf said it was time for council?

5. What was the Goblins' behavior toward their own during the onslaught?

6. Why did Bilbo stand on Ravenhill with the elves at the end of the battle?

7. In what spirit did Dain give his gifts? How did this differ from Thorin's promises?

8. What did the elf poem reveal about the hobbit's feelings?

9. What happened to Bilbo's reputation as a result of his adventures?

10. Why didn't Bilbo Baggins visit with his friends in the North?

Chapters XVII – XIX (cont.)

Questions for Discussion:

1. Do you think Thorin's quest was fulfilled? Why do you think his death was necessary? Do you think he deserved the reader's admiration?

2. Do you agree with Bilbo's thought that "he made a great mess of that business with the stone"?

Writing Activity:

A quest is a search made to secure an object or achieve a goal. In the Middle Ages an adventure undertaken by a knight or knights was called a "Quest." In what ways may Bilbo's adventures be seen as a "Quest" story? Write a short essay describing Bilbo's quest and tell how he matured during the course of his quest.

CLOZE ACTIVITY

The following passage is taken from Chapter One of the book. Read it through completely and then go back and fill in the blank spaces with words that make sense. Then you may compare your language with that of the author.

By some curious chance one morning long ago in the quiet of the world, when there was less noise and more green, and the hobbits were still numerous and prosperous, and Bilbo Baggins was standing at his door after breakfast smoking an enormous long wooden pipe that reached nearly down to his woolly toes (neatly brushed)—Gandalf came by. Gandalf! If you had _____[1] only a quarter of what I have _____[2] about him, and I have only heard _____[3] little of all there is to hear, _____[4] would be prepared for any sort of _____[5] tale. Tales and adventures sprouted up all _____[6] the place wherever he went, in the _____[7] extraordinary fashion. He had not been down _____[8] way under The Hill for ages and ages, _____[9] since his friend the Old Took died, in _____,[10] and the hobbits had almost forgotten what _____[11] looked like. He had been away _____[12] The Hill and across The Water on businesses of _____[13] own since they were all small hobbit-boys _____[14] hobbit-girls.

All that the unsuspecting Bilbo saw _____[15] morning was an old man with a _____.[16] He had a tall pointed blue hat, _____[17] long grey cloak, a silver scarf over _____[18] his long white beard hung down below his _____,[19] and immense black boots.

"Good morning!" said _____,[20] and he meant it. The sun was _____,[21] and the grass was very green. But Gandalf _____[22] at him from under long bushy _____[23] that stuck out further than the brim _____[24] his shady hat.

"What do you mean?" _____[25] said. "Do you wish me a good _____,[26] or mean that it is a good _____[27] whether I want it or not; or _____[28] you feel good this morning; or _____[29] it is a morning to be good _____?"[30]

"All of them at once," said Bilbo. "_____[31] a very fine morning for a pipe _____[32] tobacco out of doors, into the bargain. _____[33] you have a pipe about you, sit _____[34] and have a fill of mine! There's _____[35] hurry, we have all the day before _____!"[36] Then Bilbo sat down on a seat by his door, crossed his legs, and blew out a beautiful grey ring of smoke that sailed up into the air without breaking and floated away over The Hill.

POST-READING ACTIVITIES

1. Return to the Reality / Fantasy chart that you began on page five of this study guide. Record any additions you want to make to the chart. Compare your responses with those of your classmates and discuss how elements of reality were woven into this fantasy.

2. Return to the Characterization chart that you began on page nine of this study guide. Add information to the chart and compare your responses with those of your classmates.

3. **Cooperative Learning Activity:** Work with a small group of your classmates to make a list of the creatures who came to the aid of Bilbo and the dwarves in their quest. Indicated how each group helped Bilbo and why they helped.

4. Gandalf says to Bilbo and the dwarves as he leaves them at the edge of Mirkwood, "We may meet again before it is all over, and then again of course we may not. That depends on your luck and on your courage and sense . . . ." Do you think that luck or determination played a greater part in Bilbo's adventures? Cite specific examples of each and show their importance.

5. At the beginning of the tale, Tolkien remarks that, "He [Bilbo] may have lost the neighbors' respect, but he gained—well, you will see whether he gained anything in the end." Do you think he gained anything? If so, tell what he gained.

6. **Art Connection:** Choose one of the settings of the book such as Bilbo's home, Lake-town, Misty Mountain, or another one of your choice. Make a model, draw a mural, paint a picture, or create a diorama of the setting you choose.

7. Bilbo feels that the war is fought over old wounds—old feelings that are no longer valid. Why did the men and the dwarves and the elves want to fight? What differences existed between Bilbo's ideas and the ideas of the others? Was this war worth fighting? Do you think one conflict was more evil than another?

8. Tolkien has used the problem of evil as the central theme of this book. The plot and the interaction of characters was aimed at the destruction of evil. What traits did Tolkien define as "evil"? What traits did he define as "good"? Do you agree?

Post-Reading Activities (cont.)

9. Plan to view the video version of *The Hobbit*. Before you see the film, work with a partner to predict whether any scenes will be added, changed, or omitted. After you view the film, discuss why you think the changes or omissions were made. Did you prefer the book or the film?

10. **Literature Circle:** Have a literature circle discussion in which you tell your personal reactions to *The Hobbit*. Here are some questions and sentence starters to help your literature circle begin a discussion.

    • In what ways is the world of *The Hobbit* like the real world?

    • Would you like to know Bilbo Baggins? Do you think he would like to know you?

    • Which character did you like the most? The least?

    • Who else would like to read this fantasy? Why?

    • What questions would you like to ask the author?

    • It was not fair when . . .

    • I would have liked to see . . .

    • I didn't understand . . .

    • I wonder . . .

11. **Fluency—Choral Reading:** Work with a small group to read aloud any of the poems in the book. After you have selected the poem, determine which lines should be read as a chorus in unison and which lines should be read by one voice alone. Should that voice be male or female, soft or loud, high-pitched or low? Discuss whether the poem should be read slowly or quickly. Practice reading the poem together with your group before presenting it to the rest of the class.

SUGGESTIONS FOR FURTHER READING

* Babbit, Natalie. *The Search for Delicious*. Square Fish.

* _____. *Tuck Everlasting*. Square Fish.

Baum, Frank L. *The Wonderful Wizard of Oz*. Dover.

* Brittain, Bill. *The Wish Giver*. HarperCollins.

* Carroll, Lewis. *Alice's Adventures in Wonderland*. Bantam.

* Grahame, Kenneth. *Wind in the Willows*. Aladdin.

Hopkins, Lee Bennett, ed. *Elves, Fairies and Gnomes*. Knopf.

* L'Engle, Madeleine. *A Wrinkle in Time*. Square Fish.

* Lewis, C.S. *The Lion, the Witch and the Wardrobe*. HarperCollins.

* Norton, Mary. *The Borrowers*. HMS Books for Young Readers.

* O'Brien, Robert. *Mrs. Frisby and the Rats of NIMH*. Aladdin.

Rebsamen, Frederick (translator). *Beowulf*. Perennial Modern Classics.

* Rowling, J.K. *Harry Potter and the Sorcerer's Stone*. Scholastic.

* Steinbeck, John. *The Pearl*. Penguin.

Swift, Jonathan. *Gulliver's Travels*. Dover.

Some Other Books by J.R.R. Tolkien

The Adventures of Tom Bombadil. HarperCollins.

The Annotated Hobbit. HarperCollins.

Bilbo's Last Song. Knopf.

The Book of Lost Tales. Del Rey.

Farmer Giles of Ham. Unwin.

The Lord of the Rings. Mariner Books.

The Shaping of Middle Earth. Del Rey.

Bibliography for Teachers

Bettelheim, Bruno, *The Uses of Enchantment*. Vintage.

Kocher, Paul H. *Master of Middle-Earth*. Del Rey.

Noel, Ruth S. *The Mythology of Middle Earth*. Houghton Mifflin.

* NOVEL-TIES Study Guides are available for these titles.

ANSWER KEY

Chapter I

Vocabulary: 1. e 2. h 3. b 4. f 5. g 6. d 7. c 8. a; 1. audacious 2. prudent 3. legendary 4. remuneration 5. obstinately 6. haughty 7. blunder 8. fragments

Questions: 1. Gandalf came to enlist Bilbo Baggins' aid in reclaiming the dwarves' lost treasure from the dragons. He wished to hire Bilbo as Burglar on an expedition to the Lonely Mountain. 2. The wealth and collections of valuables that the dwarves in Dale amassed became known to humans and dragons. A particularly greedy dragon, called Smaug, conquered the dwarves and stole the treasure. 3. When the dwarves entered his home, it was clear that Bilbo Baggins was concerned with respectable politeness and a code of hospitality, didn't respond well to surprises, and was a little selfish. 4. The music of the dwarves aroused impetuous feelings of adventurousness in Bilbo that he inherited from his mother's family. The Tooks, whose family tree was whispered to have included a fairy, were inclined to magic, daring, and excitement, while the Baggins family was more conventional, preferring the quiet pleasures of a comfortable hole. 5. When Bilbo went in, he became angered by Gloin's insulting words: he resolved to show the dwarves that he was fearless and strong. 6. Gandalf used flattery and the intriguing revelation of secrets to confirm Bilbo's wavering resolve to join the dwarves.

Chapters II – IV

Vocabulary: 1. e 2. f 3. g 4. c 5. a 6. h 7. b 8. d; 1. shirk 2. palpitate 3. paraphernalia 4. deception 5. gnash 6. plunder 7. esteemed 8. incantations

Questions: 1. Bilbo followed the dwarves' commands because he was not prepared to argue and was flabbergasted by sharp responses from Gandalf. 2. A Hobbit, such as Bilbo, might make an excellent burglar because he could move absolutely quietly in the woods. 3. The dwarves were in great danger because they might be eaten by the trolls who captured them. 4. Gandalf took advantage of the trolls' argumentativeness by imitating their voices and thus extended their bickering until dawn when they turned to stone. 5. Bilbo wanted to stay and visit with the elves because he enjoyed their good spirits, their songs, and their gossip. 6. The expedition enjoyed Elrond's hospitality for fourteen days as they heard his tales, which imparted their history, had their clothing mended, rested their bodies, ate good food, and prepared for the continuing journey. 7. Through his knowledge of runes and moon letters, Elrond was able to decipher the origins of the two swords retrieved from the trolls and the directions for access to the secret door to the mountain. 8. The expedition took shelter in a cave as they sought protection from a storm. 9. The goblins were furious when they saw the sword Thorin had worn because they knew it had once been used in a battle in which many goblins had been killed.

Chapters V – VII

Vocabulary: 1. f 2. a 3. b 4. e 5. h 6. d 7. g 8. c; 1. trestle 2. subterranean 3. tense 4. stark 5. antique 6. morsel 7. bracken 8. appalling

Questions: 1. When he regained consciousness, Bilbo found himself in a place of intense darkness, suffering from hunger and a headache due to his head injury. 2. Bilbo played a riddle game with Gollum to prevent himself from being eaten by Gollum, the strange, lone creature in the depths. Also, if Bilbo asked a riddle that Gollum could not answer, he would be allowed to escape. 3. Bilbo learned that the ring was ancient and could magically render its wearer invisible. 4. Bilbo was able to escape because the ring made him invisible to Gollum, who inadvertently led him toward the door, and then invisible to Trolls, who would not pursue him out into the light. 5. Gandalf had a strong allegiance toward Bilbo because he felt responsible for getting him involved in the adventure. 6. Not telling the dwarves about the magic ring advanced Bilbo's reputation for cleverness, as the dwarves assumed he was visible and had managed to slip by Balin. Now the ring became a secret tool of his own, whose future use would be considerable, if not yet known. 7. The wolves fled because Gandalf tossed burning pinecones at them, sticking to their fur and causing it to combust. In fear and terror, the wolves fled. 8. Bilbo and the dwarves escaped the flaming trees by eagles summoned by Gandalf. 9. Gandalf decided it was time to leave the quest because he had only intended to accompany the party over the mountains; the dwarves' adventure was not his, and he had other pressing concerns. 10. Beorn was called a "skin-changer" because he could become a man or a bear at will. 11. Beorn was willing to help Gandalf and the others because he was impressed by Gandalf's intriguing story; then when he had verified it, he admired Gandalf's prowess in killing the Great Goblin and decimating the Wargs and escaping.

Chapters VIII – X

Vocabulary: 1. inquisitive–curious 2. vexed–bothered; annoyed 3. portcullis–strong iron grating used as gateway to a fortified palace 4. potent–powerful; strong 5. ominous–threatening evil or harm 6. enmity–hostility; bad feelings

Questions: 1. The Hobbit and the dwarves decided not to hunt, since it would be fruitless, and they also did not want to leave the path. 2. It was lucky that Bilbo realized he was being tied up in time to fight back; that he guessed where to find the captured dwarves; that he could slash through the spiders' hasty trap; and that a spider-rope was left hanging for him to reach the high branch where the dwarves were tied. 3. Killing the great spider with his sword—without any help from anyone—gave Bilbo a sense of confidence and strength. It was a moment of independent achievement in which he recognized his new mental and physical powers. 4. The Elvenking, presuming the dwarves were trying to capture his treasure, imprisoned them. 5. Thorin didn't want the Elvenking to know about his quest because he did not want to share the treasure. 6. Bilbo first burgled for food to support himself in the Elvenking's palace. 7. Bilbo's plan was to slip the dwarves out in barrels on a stream that passed under the cellar of the palace. Luck helped the scheme when the guards drank strong wine and fell asleep. 8. Gandalf decided to rejoin Bilbo when he learned that the road the dwarves and Bilbo had taken on Beorn's advice was no longer a safe route through Mirkwood. 9. The Lake-town men were excited by Thorin's mission, which had been foretold in their folktales and songs. Their business-like Master, more concerned about his relations with the Elvenking than the prophecies of old songs, disbelieved Thorin's claim of descent from Thor, King of the Mountain. 10. When the people of Lake-town clamored for the dwarves and their quest, the Master arranged for them to be fed and clothed and provided a house and boats for their use.

Chapters XI – XIII

Vocabulary: 1. waning 2. lair 3. perilous 4. marauding 5. crannies 6. pallid 7. cowered

Questions: 1. Elrond read the moon letters on Thorin's map which prophesied that if the dwarves "stand by the grey stone when the thrush knocks," the setting sun would shine on the key-hole on Durin's day when the last moon of Autumn and the sun were in the sky together. 2. After the scrapes Bilbo had gotten them out of, he expected the dwarves might explore the cave with him, but he was disappointed when none volunteered to enter the dark tunnel with him. Compared to the hobbit's emotional involvement in the quest and his streak of adventurousness, the dwarves were strict in their calculation of services and rewards. 3. When he saw the dragon-hoard of Smaug, Bilbo desired the treasure in the way the dwarves had for generations. 4. In his second encounter with the dragon, Bilbo learned about the vulnerable bare spot in Smaug's impenetrable gem-like skin—a hollow in the left breast. 5. Bilbo could not resist taking the Arkenstone; he was enchanted by its magical light. He was excited and proud of himself, but a little apprehensive about the dwarves' reactions. 6. The dwarves' ancestral treasure "rekindled all the fire of their dwarvish hearts" and emboldened them. Their marvelous armor would help to protect them, too. 7. The dwarves and Bilbo left the palace to escape the returning Smaug. Thorin and Balin knew the palace well since they had lived in it long ago before the dragon's arrival.

Chapters XIV – XVI

Vocabulary: Across—2. benefactor 5. prophecies 8. foreboding 10. bade 11. amends; Down—1. decrepit 3. eminent 4. foiled 6. laden 7. coveted 9. dreary

Questions: 1. The title "Barrel-rider" indicated to Smaug that Bilbo came from the river and received aid from the men of Lake-town. 2. Bard was able to slay the dragon because he had the ability to understand the thrush's message from the mountain and because he possessed a great black arrow. Both came down to him as a descendent of Girion, herd of Dale. 3. The Master was speaking of Thorin's company. His statement was brilliantly calculated to distract the people's attention from his cowardly retreat and Bard's heroism and to turn them to thoughts of treasure and revenge. 4. The Master was a shrewd politician, an astute businessman, and an able administrator. Bard had inherited wisdom, courage, and sureness of purpose. All of Bard's qualities contributed to his killing of Smaug. 5. With news of the death of Smaug, the Elvenking anticipated a great war and also dreamed of the unguarded wealth in the Mountain. 6. Thorin's dwarvish desire for gold made him obstinate against the claims of Bard and the Lakemen, but Bilbo's long-suppressed love of warmth, comfort, and solid meals had finally been released after Smaug's death. 7. Bombur meant that Thorin was proud and stubborn.

Chapters XVII – XIX

Vocabulary: 1. alter 2. casket 3. wrath 4. ponder 5. onslaught 6. content

Questions: 1. Thorin promised Bard a fourteenth share of the treasure in exchange for the Arkenstone. 2. Dain's army attacked first because Bard was persuaded to hesitate by the cautious Elvenking. 3. The Elvenking decided not to begin a war for gold because he hoped for some peaceful reconciliation. 4. Dain put aside the quarrel with the elves and men to fight the Goblins, a common enemy of fearful power. 5. In their haste the Goblins paid no attention to those who fell from the sharp cliffs. 6. Bilbo stood on Ravenhill with the elves at the end of the battle because there was more chance of escape from that point, and he preferred the elves to the dwarves. 7. Dain's generosity contrasted with the strictness of Thorin's contractual agreement to divide the treasure. 8. The Elves' song accurately reflected Bilbo's longing for his comfortable and familiar hearth and his weariness with travel and hardship. 9. Bilbo's respectability among the hobbits was ruined by his long adventures. 10. Bilbo did not visit his friends in the North because he was content to remain home and receive visitors after his long adventures.